The HUMAN BODY

MAKING SENSE *of* SCIENCE

Peter Riley

W
FRANKLIN WATTS
LONDON • SYDNEY

First published in 2004 by Franklin Watts
96 Leonard Street, London EC2A 4XD

Franklin Watts Australia
45-51 Huntley Street, Alexandria, NSW 2015

Text copyright © Peter Riley 2004
Design and concept © Franklin Watts 2004

Series Editor: Rachel Cooke
Editor: Kate Newport
Art director: Jonathan Hair
Designer: Mo Choy

Picture credits:
AJ Photo/SPL: 13b.
Ancient Art & Architecture Collection/Topham: 17b.
Bettmann/Corbis: 9t, 11c. BSIP, Laurent/SPL: 29cl.
Dr Jeremy Burgess/SPL: 15b. CC Studio/SPL: 28b.
Pr S.Cinti/CNRI /SPL: 6bl. CNRI/SPL: 7br.
Adam Hart-Davis/SPL: 7cl, 7bl.
Pascal Goetgheluck/SPL: 29tr.
Sally Greenhill/S & R Greenhill: 20, 21.
Image Works/Topham: 25t. Coneyl Jay/SPL: 28c.
Nancy Kedersha /UCLA /SPL: 19bl.
Dr Kari Lounatmaa/SPL: front cover inset.
Moredun Scientiflic Ltd/SPL: 25b. Dr G. Moscoso/SPL: 23c.
Prof. P. Motta/Dept. of Anatomy /University "La Sapienza", Rome/SPL: 6br.
Chris Priest & Mark Clarke/SPL: 27t.
J.C. Revy/SPL: 11b. Galen Rowell/Corbis: front cover main.
Sovereign, ISM/SPL: 5. SPL: 17bl, 27b.
Dr Linda Stannard, UCT/SPL: 24t, 24c.
VVG/SPL: 16cr.

Picture research: Diana Morris

All other photography by Ray Moller.

Every attempt has been made to clear copyright.
Should there be any inadvertent omission,
please apply to the publisher for rectification.

A CIP catalogue record for this book
is available from the British Library

ISBN 0 7496 5528 3

Printed in Malaysia

CONTENTS

WHAT HAPPENS INSIDE THE BODY?

Stand or sit still – you might say that you are 'doing nothing'. But under the skin your body is always busy. The heart pumps blood around the body. The skeleton supports you, while the muscles work with the senses to keep you balanced. The lungs take in new air and push old air out. The digestive system breaks down food so that you can get nutrients from it.

The body is made up of many different organs, each with a different task. The organs work together in groups called organ systems. There are eleven organ systems.

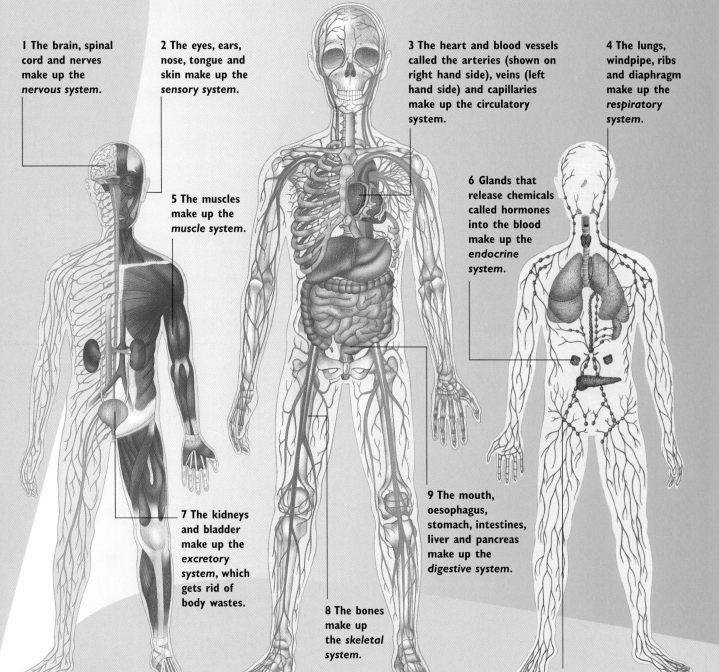

1 The brain, spinal cord and nerves make up the *nervous system.*

2 The eyes, ears, nose, tongue and skin make up the *sensory system.*

3 The heart and blood vessels called the arteries (shown on right hand side), veins (left hand side) and capillaries make up the circulatory system.

4 The lungs, windpipe, ribs and diaphragm make up the *respiratory system.*

5 The muscles make up the *muscle system.*

6 Glands that release chemicals called hormones into the blood make up the *endocrine system.*

7 The kidneys and bladder make up the *excretory system*, which gets rid of body wastes.

8 The bones make up the *skeletal system.*

9 The mouth, oesophagus, stomach, intestines, liver and pancreas make up the *digestive system.*

10 The *immune system* protects us from disease.

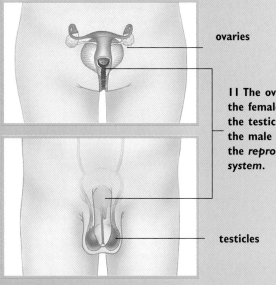

ovaries

11 The ovaries in the female and the testicles in the male make up the *reproductive system*.

testicles

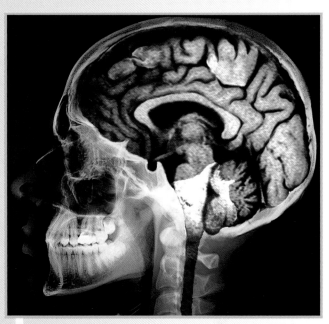

This scan of the head shows the position of the brain. The folded part across the top is called the cerebrum. It has many functions. You are using yours right now to understand the picture.

HOW HEAVY ARE YOUR BONES AND MUSCLES?

Work out the mass (weight) of your bones and muscles. Bones make up 15 per cent of your body mass and muscles make up about 45 per cent. Weigh yourself and find your mass in kilograms. Now work out the mass of your bones and muscles in the following way:

• Mass of your bones = your total mass (e.g. 40 kg) x 15/100 = (e.g. 6 kg).

• Mass of your muscles = your total mass (e.g. 40 kg) x 45/100 = (e.g. 18 kg)

CLAUDIUS GALEN

Galen (about AD 129–216) was a Greek doctor who was interested in how the insides of the body were arranged. During his life it was forbidden to cut up human bodies, so instead he cut up the bodies of apes and other animals. He supposed that the human body was arranged in a similar way to these animals, but some of his ideas were later shown to be untrue.

LOOKING INSIDE THE BODY

Scientists and doctors have worked together for hundreds of years to learn about the body and how it works. An important part of this knowledge has come from dissecting (cutting open) dead bodies. The knowledge gained from dissections has made it possible for surgeons to operate safely on living people.

Today we have ways of looking inside the body without cutting it open. X-rays, for instance, pass through most body organs but are stopped by bones and teeth. By photographing the body with X-rays it is possible to see the bones or teeth inside the flesh.

Other machines called scanners can take a detailed picture of a slice through the body, using either X-rays or magnetism and radio waves. Doctors can use such scans to help diagnose a patient's illness.

THE BODY'S BUILDING BLOCKS

The human body is made of tiny packets of life called cells. About 200 cells would fit into the full stop at the end of this sentence, and the human body contains up to 65 billion of them.

There are many different kinds of cell in the body but they all have the same three basic features: a nucleus, cytoplasm and a cell membrane.

The *cell membrane* holds in the cytoplasm and the nucleus. There are tiny holes in it called pores. These control the movement of substances into and out of the cell.

The *nucleus* is the control centre of the cell. It contains all the information that the cell needs to grow properly and carry out its tasks.

The *cytoplasm* is a thin jelly-like substance, similar to wallpaper paste. It contains a variety of tiny structures that work together to keep the cell alive.

DIFFERENT TYPES OF CELLS

Certain cells are designed to perform particular tasks. For example, muscle cells are long and thin. They contain tiny threads that can slide over each other to make the cell contract (get shorter). Because muscles are made from many muscle cells, when the muscle cells shorten the whole muscle contracts and brings about movement.

Another kind of cell lines your windpipe. These cells have tiny hairs called cilia, which can wave backwards and forwards. The cilia are covered in a layer of sticky mucus, which traps dust from the air. The waving action of the cilia moves the dust and mucus to the back of your mouth, where you swallow it.

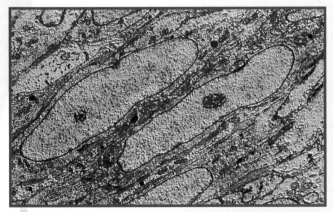

Smooth muscle cells are spindle shaped. They are wider in the centre and thinner towards each end.

These are cells that line and protect the windpipe. They are covered in tiny hairs or cilia.

WATCH YOUR IRIS SHRINK

The iris of the eye is made of long, thin muscle cells. Muscles running in a ring round the iris can contract to shrink the pupil and let less light into the eye. Muscles that radiate out like spokes in a wheel can contract to open the pupil and let in more light.

Set up a light by a mirror then cover your eyes with your hand for two minutes. Now open your eyes and look in the mirror. What happens to the pupil?

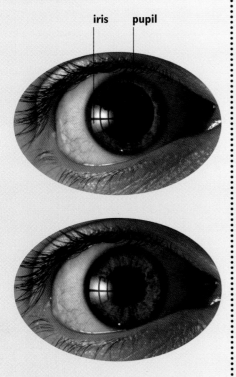

iris   pupil

The pupil contracts when you open your eyes so that too much light does not reach the sensitive retina at the back of the eye.

CELLS, TISSUES AND ORGANS

In the same way that many muscle cells are organised together into muscles, other kinds of cell do not work alone but combine together in large numbers to form tissues. Muscles are one kind of tissue. Another is epithelium (cells that cover a surface, such as the cells lining the windpipe).

Groups of tissues develop next to each other to form organs. For example, the stomach contains tissues that produce digestive juices and muscular tissues that churn up the food.

STAINING CELLS

Most human body cells are colourless and this makes them difficult to see under the microscope. In 1856 an English chemist called William Perkin (1838–1907) discovered that dyes could be made from substances in coal tar. Other scientists, such as Paul Ehrlich (1854–1915), a German scientist, began experimenting with the dyes and found that they could be used to stain the different parts of a cell and make them easier to see.

CANCERS

Cancers are caused by cells that have something wrong with the nucleus, that makes them grow uncontrollably. This forms a lump called a tumour. If a patient is found to have a lump that might be cancer, cells may be taken from it and examined under a microscope to see if they are cancer cells.

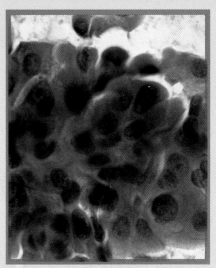

Cancer cells have a different appearance to normal cells and can be identified by examining tissues with a microscope.

HOW DO WE KEEP GOING?

Food provides the body with important substances called nutrients. The body can use nutrients to make the materials needed for new cells. Nutrients also provide the energy to keep cells alive. There are six groups of nutrients.

protein and fat

fat

protein and carbohydrate

fibre, carbohydrate and vitamins

fibre, protein and minerals

protein, minerals and fat

1. PROTEINS

Proteins provide materials for making and repairing cells and are needed for growth. They also make hormones (see pages 20 and 21) and enzymes (see page 10). Meat, fish, peas, beans, cereals, cheese and milk are foods rich in protein.

2. FATS

Fats provide materials for making cell membranes and an insulating layer under the skin to help keep the body warm. They also provide energy. Meats, nuts, hard cheese and cream are all foods rich in fat.

TEST FOR FAT

Make a collection of different foods. Rub each one on a piece of white paper and leave the paper for a while to allow any water to dry. Hold the paper up to a window or lamp. If you can see light through the rub mark, the food contains fat.

3. CARBOHYDRATES

Carbohydrates provide energy. Sugars are simple types of carbohydrate. Foods such as rice, pasta, bread, potatoes and fruits are also rich in carbohydrates.

4. MINERALS

Minerals are needed for many purposes in the body. Iron is needed to make red blood cells and calcium is needed to make bone and help muscles work. Meat, eggs, milk, cheese, spinach and green vegetables are all mineral-rich foods.

5. VITAMINS

Vitamins help the body grow healthily and protect it from disease. Foods rich in vitamins include carrots, tomatoes, milk and butter, blackcurrants, oranges, potatoes and cabbage.

6. FIBRE

Fibre helps muscles in the stomach and intestines push the food through the digestive system and prevents constipation. Fibre is found in food such as cereals, cabbage, beans and peas.

FINDING THE NUTRIENTS

Look at your evening meal and decide which foods are rich in each of the six different kinds of nutrients. Is your meal providing them all?

James Lind first worked as a surgeon's mate in the British Navy when he became a doctor. He went on to run a navy hospital and showed that scurvy was due to a poor diet.

In the 18th century a disease called scurvy was common among sailors. In scurvy the blood vessels break down, causing bleeding in the gums, in joints and inside the body. In some cases it can cause death. A Scottish doctor called James Lind (1716–1794) believed that scurvy was common in sailors because of their diet of meat broth, porridge and biscuits. When he tried adding other foods to the diet he found that citrus fruits such as limes and lemons prevented scurvy. Today we know that these foods contain vitamin C, which is needed to keep blood vessels healthy.

THE **FOOD PYRAMID**

We do not need the same amount of all the nutrients. For example we only need a small amount of fat – eating too much can damage health. An easy way to remember the quantities of nutrients to eat is to use a food pyramid like the one shown here. We need only small amounts of foods at the top of the pyramid, but large amounts of foods at the base of the pyramid.

BREAKING DOWN FOOD

The nutrients in food cannot pass directly to the cells where they are needed. Our bodies must first digest the food (break it down) to release the nutrients. Then they must pass out of the digestive system and into the blood, which carries them to the cells.

Digestion takes place in the digestive system – your gut, or alimentary canal. Take a trip along the alimentary canal by following the numbered captions in this picture.

1 Food enters through the *mouth* and is chewed into small pieces by the teeth. Saliva produced in the mouth starts breaking down carbohydrates in the food.

2 Taste buds on the *tongue* help us to taste the food. The tongue then pushes the food to the back of the mouth.

3 Muscles produce a wave of movement along the *oesophagus* that pushes food into the stomach.

4 The *stomach* releases acid to kill germs, and starts to break down protein. The stomach also churns the food to mix it up.

liver

5 In the *duodenum*, the gall bladder releases bile onto the food. The bile breaks up fat into tiny drops.

6 The *pancreas* releases enzymes that break down proteins, fats and carbohydrates so that they dissolve.

7 In the *small intestine* all the nutrients pass through the intestine wall and into the blood.

8 In the *large intestine* water is taken back into the blood to be used again to make saliva and other juices.

9 The *rectum* stores undigested food such as fibre and releases it through the anus.

BILE IN ACTION

The bile released from the duodenum breaks fats in the food into tiny droplets, which are easier to digest. You can see how this works using washing-up liquid. Put a few drops of cooking oil in a beaker of water and stir it up. How big are the fat drops? Now add a few drops of washing-up liquid and stir again. How big are the drops now?

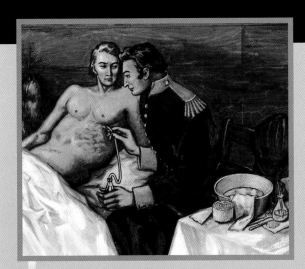

After Alexis St Martin was shot in the stomach he recovered to full health except for a hole in his stomach. This helped William Beaumont to make discoveries about digestion.

TESTING DIGESTION

William Beaumont (1785–1853), an American surgeon, saved the life of Alexis St Martin, who had been shot in the stomach. At the end of the operation Beaumont was unable to close the wound completely, and a hole was left in the stomach. Beaumont carried out several experiments in which he put samples of food on string into St Martin's stomach and pulled them out later to see how the stomach had treated them. He found, for instance, that vegetables took longer to digest than meat, and that the stomach juices needed to be warm to break down food.

LOOKING AT DIGESTION

Barium is a metal but it can take part in many chemical reactions to make a range of compounds. One compound, called barium sulphate, is particularly useful as it can move harmlessly through the alimentary canal yet stops X-rays passing through it. This makes it possible to look at the alimentary canal. A patient eats a meal of barium sulphate (called a barium meal) before the alimentary canal is X-rayed.

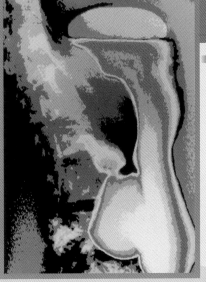

This x-ray shows the stomach after a barium meal.

BREATHING FOR ENERGY

People tend to think of respiration as breathing but it is really something else. Breathing is the changing of gases in the lungs. Respiration is the release of energy from food and it takes place in every cell in the body. Every minute of the day our lungs need to take in fresh air and push stale air out. Our lungs are moving oxygen into the body and carbon dioxide out. The blood then carries these between the lungs and the cells.

1 We breathe air in and out through the nose. The nasal passages filter dust from incoming air and warm and moisten it. Dust, dry air and cold air can all damage lung tissues.

2 Rings of stiff cartilage in the windpipe keep it open all the time. Cells with tiny hairs (cilia) move dust away from the lungs to be swallowed (see page 6).

3 The windpipe divides into two bronchi (air tubes), one going to each lung.

4 If you look closely at the lungs you can see how the bronchi divide many times to form millions of tiny air tubes. At the end of each tube is an air pocket.

6 The diaphragm separates the chest from the abdomen. It moves up and down to make a pumping action to change the air in the lungs.

5 If you look closer still, you can see the blood flowing in the walls of the air pockets. It picks up oxygen from the air and takes it to the cells. The blood also releases waste carbon dioxide into the lungs. The millions of air pockets enable these gases to enter and leave the body very quickly.

blood vessels

air pockets

SQUASH UP A SURFACE AREA

If the lungs were unfolded they would make an area the size of a tennis court. An A3 sheet of tissue paper is about 800 times smaller than the area of the lungs. Try screwing an A3 sheet into as small a ball as possible. If you can pack it tight enough to fit on a tablespoon, the paper will be as tightly packed as the tissues in the lungs (a tablespoon is around 800 times smaller than the space in your chest).

CHANGING THE AIR

The pumping action of the respiratory system is called ventilation. Raising the ribs and lowering the diaphragm expands the lungs and pulls air into them.

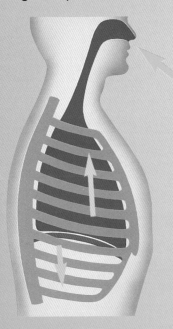

Lowering the ribs and raising the diaphragm pushes air out of the lungs.

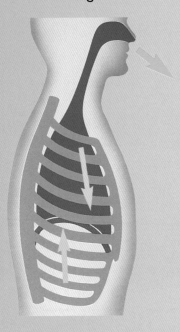

When the early scientists made their dissections they did not always understand what they saw. Galen, for example, believed that there was a life spirit in the air. He thought that when the air was breathed in, it passed into the windpipe then into a vein close to the heart and then into the heart itself. From here the life spirit travelled in the blood to the brain then changed into animal spirit, which moved down the nerves and made the body move.

This is an early statue of Galen. He was one of the first thinkers to use dissections to test out his ideas.

LUNG DISEASE

Sometimes scientists don't do experiments to draw conclusions, they just collect data and study it.

This patient is suffering from a disease brought on by smoking. He is using special equipment to help him breathe.

The link between smoking and lung disease was discovered this way. When data was collected on details of people who died from lung disease, it was found that many of them had been smokers. Further studies showed that most people who died of lung cancer were also smokers. The link between smoking and cancer was finally made when experiments were done on tobacco smoke. They showed that there were chemicals in the smoke that caused the cancers.

13

THE HEART AND BLOOD

The circulatory system is made up of the heart, the blood vessels and the blood itself. The blood is the body's transport system. It carries essential substances to the cells and takes away their wastes. The pumping action of the heart moves the blood around the body.

It takes about 45 seconds for the blood to make one complete circuit of the circulatory system.

THE HEART

Your heart is a bag of muscle about the size of your fist. The muscle is called cardiac muscle and contracts regularly throughout your life. The heart is basically two pumps, side by side. Each pump has two valves, which let the blood move through them one way but not the other. As the pumps work the valves open and close, making the sounds we call heartbeats.

The heart has four chambers, two to each pump.

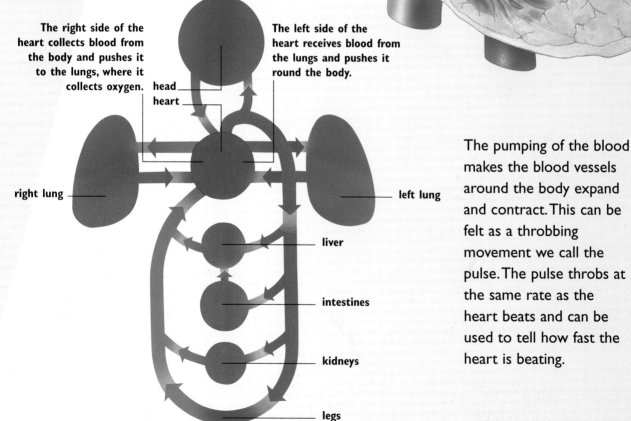

The right side of the heart collects blood from the body and pushes it to the lungs, where it collects oxygen.

The left side of the heart receives blood from the lungs and pushes it round the body.

head
heart

right lung

left lung

liver

intestines

kidneys

legs

The pumping of the blood makes the blood vessels around the body expand and contract. This can be felt as a throbbing movement we call the pulse. The pulse throbs at the same rate as the heart beats and can be used to tell how fast the heart is beating.

CAN YOU TAKE YOUR PULSE?

Hold out your right hand with the palm up. Put your left thumb under your right wrist and use two fingers of your left hand to feel the flesh on the top of your right wrist. When you press down you will feel the throbbing of the pulse.

Count the number of times your pulse throbs in fifteen seconds and multiply by four to find how fast the heart is beating in a minute. Run around for two minutes then take your pulse again. How has your heartbeat changed?

MOVING SUBSTANCES AROUND

The blood carries oxygen from the lungs and nutrients from the small intestine to all the body's cells. It takes away their wastes too. One waste product is carbon dioxide, which the blood takes to the lungs. Another is a substance called urea, which is produced by cells in the liver as they break down protein that the body does not need. The urea is carried in the blood to the kidneys, where it forms part of your urine.

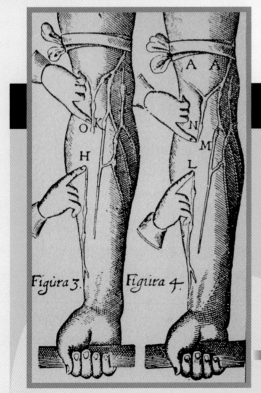

WHAT **MAKES** THE **BLOOD MOVE?**

Until the 17th century no-one understood how the circulation worked. William Harvey (1578–1657) was one of the royal physicians (doctors) to James I and Charles I of England. He spent many years studying the circulation of animals. In 1628 he published a famous book, *On the Motion of the Heart and Blood in Animals*, in which he showed that the heart acted as a pump to move the blood round the body.

This woodcut by Harvey shows the valves in the superficial veins of the forearm. On the left, for example, the finger has been passed along the vein from O to H (away from the heart).

BONES AND MUSCLES

Your bones join together to make the skeleton – the body's 'scaffolding'. The skeleton is a framework for the muscles, which provide the power of movement. However, two types of muscle are not attached to bone. They are smooth muscles like those in the iris (see page 7) and cardiac muscle (see page 14).

skull

shoulder joint

ribcage

arm bones

spine

vertebrae

pelvis

hip joint

leg bones

kneecap

LIVING BONES

We tend to think of bones as being lifeless, because we usually only see them in skeletons. But our bones contain living cells. Some of these cells use substances from our food, such as calcium, to make the hard material we call bone. The centre of some bones contains bone marrow, where blood cells are produced.

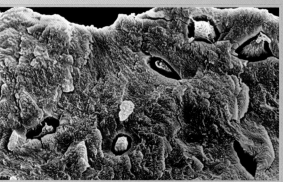

These are bone cells viewed under a microscope. They become surrounded by the bony material they produce.

HOW BONES HELP

The skeleton supports all the soft parts of the body. If the bones were not present the other organs would squash each other and stop working. Bones also provide extra protection for important organs. For example, the brain is enclosed in the bones of the skull, and the heart and lungs are protected by the ribcage.

JOINED BY JOINTS

Bones are not all rigidly fixed together, but have joints that allow movement. Joints such as the hip and shoulder can move a great deal in many directions. Knee and elbow joints can move back and forth, while joints in the skull and pelvis hardly move at all.

OILING THE JOINTS

If the bones in a joint rubbed against each other they would soon wear down.

cartilage

synovial fluid

So in joints that move a lot, the ends of the bones are capped with hard-wearing cartilage, and a liquid called synovial fluid. This is produced to oil the joints and reduce friction.

WORKING IN PAIRS

We have seen (page 6) how tiny threads inside muscle cells slide over each other to make the muscles contract (shorten). However, when a muscle relaxes it cannot lengthen on its own; the threads have to be pulled apart. So muscles are arranged in pairs that work together. One muscle pair are the biceps and triceps in the upper arm.

When the biceps contracts it stretches the triceps, which lengthens.

When the triceps contracts it stretches the biceps.

The muscles are attached to the bones by tough cords called tendons.

FIND YOUR TENDONS

Your fingers are connected to the muscles that move them by long tendons. Look at the back of your hand and stretch the fingers. You should be able to see or feel the tendons running from the fingers down the back of the hand. Can you find the muscles that these tendons are attached to? Now try feeling for the tendons on the inside of your elbows and at the back of your knees.

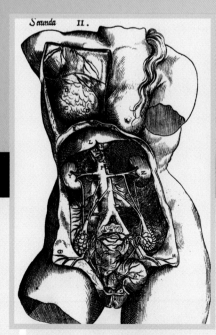

This is an anatomical diagram drawn by Vesalius in the 16th century. It shows the female form.

VESALIUS

Andreas Vesalius (1514–1564) was a Flemish (Belgian) scientist. He lived at a time when the dissection of human bodies was allowed and he repeated Galen's animal dissections in humans (see page 5). He found many inaccuracies in Galen's work. Vesalius decided to make dissections of the human body and then drew pictures of them. These beautiful and accurate drawings were used by others who were investigating the human body.

THE BRAIN AND NERVES

Our senses give us information about the world around us. They send information to the brain, which is the control centre of the nervous system. The brain may store this information in the memory, process it by comparing it with what the person already knows, or use it to send out messages of its own to other parts of the body.

LIGHTRAYS

retina

lens

image

nerves to brain

Different senses are designed to pick up different kinds of information. The eyes for example can detect light waves, while the ears pick up sound waves. Inside each sense organ the information is changed into tiny bursts of electricity, called nerve impulses. These pass along nerves to the brain.

Light from something you see gets bent by the lens to form an image on the retina at the back of the eye. Nerves then carry messages about the picture to the brain.

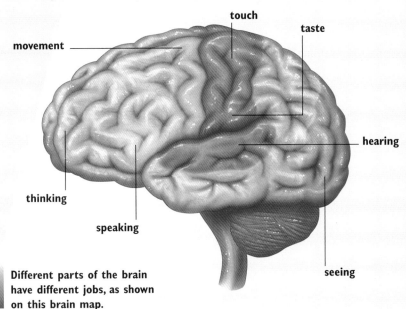

movement

touch

taste

hearing

thinking

speaking

seeing

Different parts of the brain have different jobs, as shown on this brain map.

The brain 'makes sense' of the nerve impulses from the various senses. For instance, images sent to the brain from the eyes are upside down, but the brain turns them the right way up. If a ball is being thrown to you, the brain will quickly send out messages to the muscles in your arms and hands so that you can catch it.

RECORDING THE BRAIN

In 1929 the German psychiatrist Hans Berger (1873–1941) showed that it was possible to record the electrical activity of the brain on a chart, using electrodes attached to the outside of the skull. He did this with a machine he called an electroencephalograph, or EEG. Today EEGs are used in hospitals around the world to diagnose brain disorders such as epilepsy.

HOW FAST CAN MESSAGES TRAVEL THROUGH YOUR NERVOUS SYSTEM?

Find out how fast electrical messages travel from your eye to your brain and then to your hand. Hold out your hand with your thumb and fingers about 6 centimetres apart. Ask a friend to hold a ruler above your hand so that the lower end is just between your thumb and fingers. Tell your friend to let go of the ruler whenever they want. As they drop the ruler, try and catch it. If only a small length of the ruler falls before you catch it, messages have travelled fast from your eye to your brain and hand. If you fail to catch the ruler, the messages have travelled slowly.

connections to other nerves or muscles

cell body

CELLS OF THE NERVOUS SYSTEM

Nerves are made up of many nerve cells, which have long, thin fibres that carry the nerve impulses. The end of each nerve cell connects to one or more other nerve cells, or to a muscle.

nerve fibre

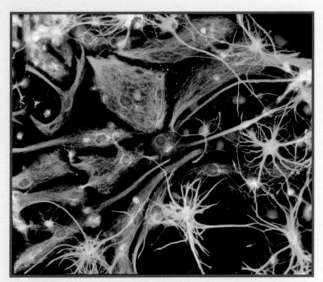

In the brain each nerve cell is connected to many others. Nerve impulses pass around whole group of brain cells to help us think and remember things.

THE **EFFECTS** OF **ALCOHOL** AND **DRUGS**

Scientific investigations have shown that drinking large amounts of alcohol or taking drugs can damage the nervous system and cause illnesses. Alcohol, for example, slows down the speed at which the nervous system can send its messages. This makes a person react more slowly to changes around them and increases the risk of them having an accident.

GROWING AND CHANGING

If you look at photographs of a person at different ages, you can see how they have grown and changed. We grow by our cells dividing to form more cells. How we grow is controlled by chemicals in the body called hormones. What we eat also affects how we grow.

Growth is easy to see — a person increases in height and weight. Growth can also cause changes. As the bones of the skull grow, they cause the face to change. For example, a baby may have a round face but as the person grows the shape of the face may change from round to oval.

At six months old.

At 10 years old.

CELLS DIVIDING

The body grows by cell division — a single cell divides to make two new ones.

The nucleus of the cell divides first.

Next, a groove develops in the cell membrane.

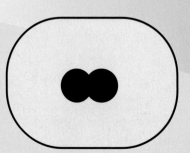

HOW FAST DOES YOUR THUMBNAIL GROW?

Cut your thumbnail and measure the distance from the base of the nail to the cut edge. A week later measure again and see how much the nail has grown.

At 20 years old.

The groove deepens and eventually separates the cytoplasm to form two cells.

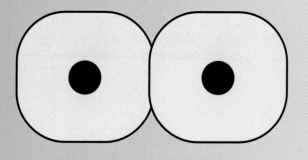

HORMONES AND GROWTH

There is an organ on the underside of the brain called the pituitary gland. It makes chemicals called hormones and releases them into the blood through the glands that make up the endocrine system. One hormone is called growth hormone. This passes round the body and makes the cells divide and organs grow. When a person reaches the age of about twelve, the sex organs – the ovaries in females and the testicles in males – also begin to produce hormones. The hormone produced by the ovaries causes the breasts to develop and the hips to widen. The hormone produced by the testicles makes the voice "break" (deepen) and causes the testicles and penis to grow bigger.

You can begin to see these changes if you look at photographs of you and your friends and family at different ages. The panel on the left shows the same person at three different stages in their life.

BABY MILK

Babies are normally fed on breast milk for the early part of their life. As well as providing all the food a baby needs, the milk provides antibodies to help protect the baby against disease (see page 26). However, many young babies also drink a synthetic kind of milk sold as a powder. Much research has been carried out to make sure that this milk gives babies everything they need for healthy growth.

MAKING NEW LIFE

A new human being grows from a single cell, called a zygote. Unlike all other cells, a zygote is made when two cells join, rather than by a cell dividing in two. The two cells that combine are a sperm cell from the father and an egg cell from the mother.

The zygote then divides and begins to grow inside its mother, using food and oxygen from her blood. After nine months, a new baby is born.

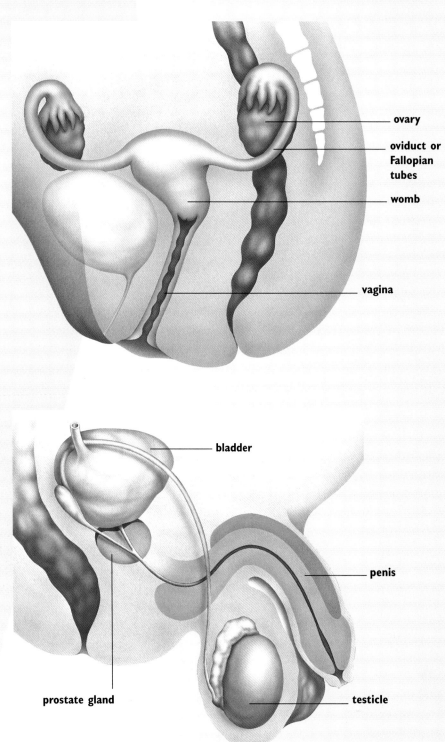

ovary

oviduct or Fallopian tubes

womb

vagina

bladder

penis

prostate gland

testicle

REPRODUCTIVE ORGANS

Males and females each have special organs for reproduction. Females have two ovaries that produce egg cells. These are connected by tubes (oviducts or Fallopian tubes) to the womb, which is connected to the outside by a passage called the vagina.

In males, the reproductive organs are two testicles, which produce sperm cells. These are connected by tubes to the prostrate gland and the penis.

HOW SEX CELLS MEET

The sex cells (the sperm and egg cells) reach each other in the following way. Sperm cells pass from the testicles along a tube leading to the penis. On the way they mix with a liquid called semen that gives them energy to swim. In sexual intercourse, sperm cells are released into the vagina by the penis. The sperm swim into the womb and from there to the oviducts. Egg cells made in the ovaries are also released into the oviducts where they meet with sperm cells.

FERTILISATION

When a sperm and an egg cell meet, the two nuclei fuse (join) to form the zygote. This process is called fertilisation.

egg cell

egg cell nucleus

sperm cells

sperm cell nucleus

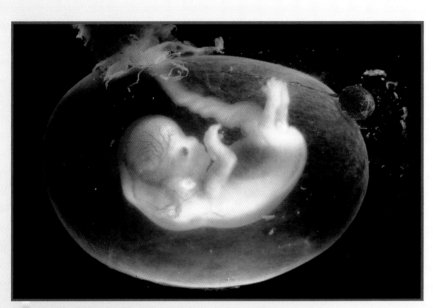

A bag of liquid called the amniotic fluid develops around the fetus to protect it while it is in the womb.

IN THE WOMB

The newly formed zygote divides several times to form a ball of cells. This then moves from the oviduct into the womb, where it attaches itself to the wall. One part of the ball forms the fetus (the developing baby). The other part forms an organ called the placenta. The placenta receives nutrients and oxygen from the mother's blood, and passes them to the fetus. It also receives wastes from the fetus and passes them into the mother's blood.

HOW DOES AMNIOTIC FLUID PROTECT THE FETUS?

Make a Plasticine model of a baby. Put it in a plastic bag (the womb), and fasten it up with some air trapped inside. Shake the bag – what happens to the baby? Now fill the bag with water and close it again. What happens when you shake the bag now?

GABRIEL FALLOPIUS

Gabriel Fallopius, (1523–1562), an Italian scientist, was taught by Vesalius (see page 17). He went on to make dissections and discoveries of his own. He was the first to identify the tubes (oviducts) connecting the ovaries to the womb. In honour of his discovery the oviducts are often called Fallopian tubes.

MICROBES AND DISEASE

Tiny organisms called micro-organisms, or microbes, can invade the body. When they do, they can cause disease. There are four kinds of microbes – bacteria, viruses, fungi and protists.

BACTERIA

Bacteria are even smaller than human cells. Many kinds of bacteria live on the outside of the body and in the digestive tract without causing us any harm. Some even help to break down food. However, a few types of bacteria can cause serious diseases such as cholera, typhoid and tuberculosis.

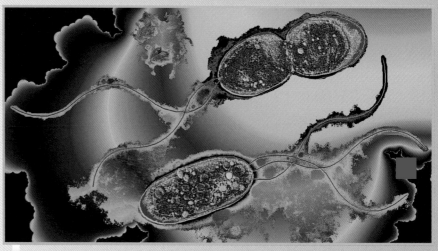

Different bacteria have distinctive shapes. Some are rod-shaped, others are rounded. These bacteria have long, whip-like hairs that they use to move.

TOOTH DECAY

Investigations on bacteria in the mouth have shown that some feed on sugar in foods and make acids, which cause tooth decay. Sweet snacks contain large amounts of sugar, which the bacteria can feed on. By switching to snacks low in sugar, like raw carrots or celery, people can reduce their chances of tooth decay.

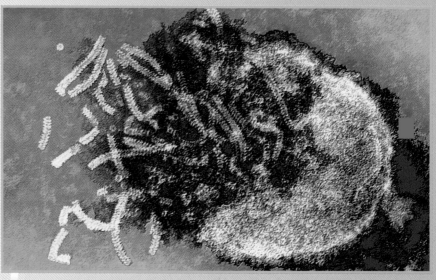

These tiny structures are viruses exploding from an infected cell. They can breed rapidly in a body, causing disease and sometimes death.

VIRUSES

Viruses are even smaller than bacteria: they can only be seen by using a powerful electron microscope. Viruses cause diseases such as the common cold, influenza and chickenpox. Viruses are made of an outer layer of protein and an inner core of DNA (the genetic material of living things). Viruses cannot grow or reproduce on their own. They must infect another living cell and take control. The virus puts the cell's machinery to work making copies of itself. Eventually the cell bursts and releases thousands more viruses.

FUNGI

Fungi are less common on the body than bacteria and viruses. However some kinds can settle on damp skin and feed on it. Gym changing rooms and swimming baths are places where you may pick up a disease called athlete's foot. This is caused by a fungus and produces cracked and sore skin between the toes.

CHECKING FOR SPORES

Fungi produces tiny 'seeds' called spores, which can travel on the gentlest of air currents. See if there are any fungal spores in the air in your room. Leave a piece of damp bread in your room for an hour, then seal it in a plastic bag. Look at the bread every day for a few days. If there were fungal spores in the air, mould will form on the bread.

PROTISTS

Most protists have a body made from a single cell and live either in freshwater or in the sea. A few are parasites living in people or animals. Some, such as the parasite that causes malaria, live part of their life in one animal and part of their life in another.

The microscope helped Pasteur show that some disease were caused by microbes.

Louis Pasteur (1822–1895), a French scientist, investigated substances such as wine and broth to find out why they went bad. Looking at them under a microscope, he found that it was due to the presence of microbes. He suggested that diseases were caused by microbes and that some may be passed from one person to another through coughs, sneezes or touch. Later work by other scientists showed that Pasteur's ideas were correct.

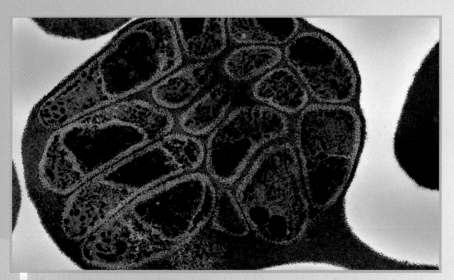

Malaria parasites live in mosquitoes and in humans. They invade human red blood cells and destroy them as this magnified image shows.

FIGHTING DISEASE

The body has a variety of defences against any microbes that try to invade it. These together make up the immune system. Sometimes microbes break through the defences and cause disease, but even then the body may eventually destroy the microbes and return to full health. Medicines and vaccines have been developed to help and to give extra protection.

LINES OF DEFENCE

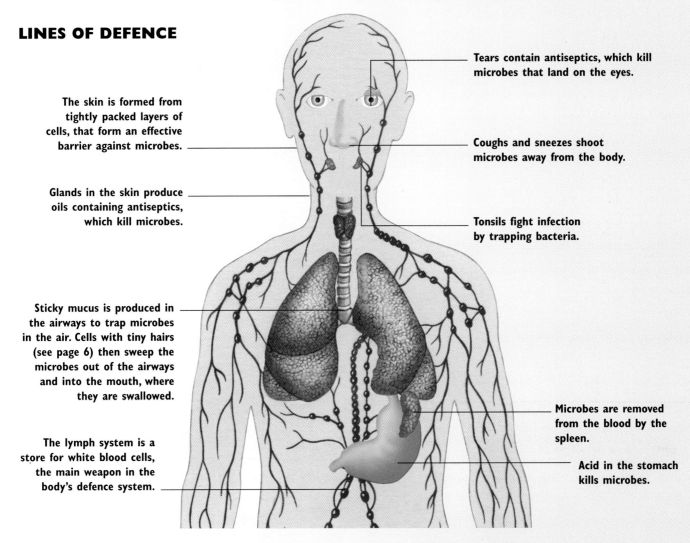

The skin is formed from tightly packed layers of cells, that form an effective barrier against microbes.

Glands in the skin produce oils containing antiseptics, which kill microbes.

Sticky mucus is produced in the airways to trap microbes in the air. Cells with tiny hairs (see page 6) then sweep the microbes out of the airways and into the mouth, where they are swallowed.

The lymph system is a store for white blood cells, the main weapon in the body's defence system.

Tears contain antiseptics, which kill microbes that land on the eyes.

Coughs and sneezes shoot microbes away from the body.

Tonsils fight infection by trapping bacteria.

Microbes are removed from the blood by the spleen.

Acid in the stomach kills microbes.

WHITE BLOOD CELLS

If microbes get past the body's first lines of defence and into the blood, they are attacked by white blood cells. Some white blood cells can engulf ('swallow') microbes. Other white cells produce antibodies. These are substances that attach to microbes and make them stick together. They can then be engulfed by white blood cells. There are many different antibodies. Each one is effective against a particular type of microbe.

MEDICINES

Medicines have been developed to defend the body against all kinds of microbe attack. Antiseptic creams are used to kill microbes of all kinds around a cut. There are also many drugs that work against microbes, such as antibiotics (drugs that kill bacteria), antiviral agents and antifungal drugs.

VACCINES

Vaccines are used to make the body safe from the attack of certain microbes. A vaccine contains dead or weakened microbes or the poisons they make. The body reacts to an injection of these substances by making antibodies, which can attack the live microbes if they enter the body. This prevents the disease from developing.

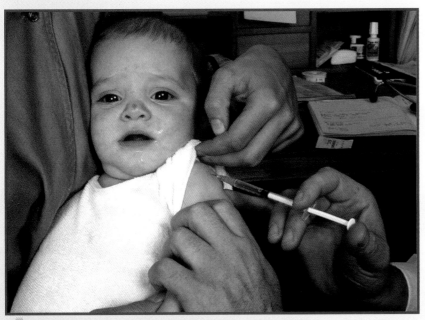

This vaccine will give protection against a deadly disease.

DISCOVERING VACCINES

An English doctor called Edward Jenner (1749–1823) noticed that milkmaids seemed to be immune to smallpox. He then discovered that the milkmaids caught a much milder disease, cowpox, from the cattle that they milked. Jenner thought that the milkmaids were immune to smallpox because they had had cowpox. To test this idea he vaccinated a boy, James Phipps, with cowpox germs, then vaccinated him with smallpox germs. The boy did not get smallpox – he had become immune. Jenner's work led to the development of vaccines against diseases such as mumps, measles and polio and the virtual eradication of smallpox.

Contemporary cartoon of Edward Jenner vaccinating eight-year-old James Phipps.

KEEPING HEALTHY

Today, we know an enormous amount about the human body. For instance, we understand that our bodies are made up of billions of tiny cells. We know that our skeleton holds us up, our muscles make us move, our nerves carry messages and our digestive system breaks down food. Doctors have learned that microbes cause many diseases. They have drugs to help cure some diseases, and vaccines to prevent others.

PREVENTING ILLNESS

Doctors today use their knowledge of the human body to help prevent illness. For instance doctors can help to reduce a patient's chances of getting heart disease by giving them regular check ups and getting them to change their lifestyle. Medical research has shown that regular exercise and cutting down on fatty foods are both ways of helping prevent heart disease.

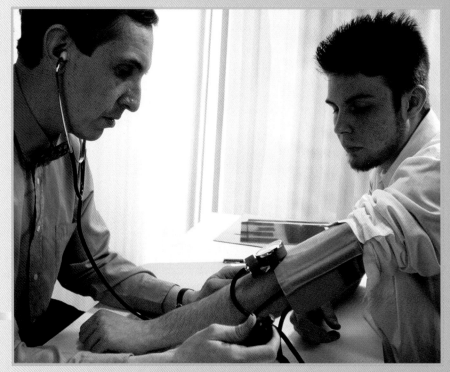

This doctor is checking a patient's blood pressure. High blood pressure can indicate heart disease and various other illnesses.

CURING DISEASE

Medical research has greatly improved the treatment of many diseases. For instance, today many cancer sufferers have a much better chance of survival than they did thirty years ago. Regular check-ups mean that cancers are now detected much earlier, before they become impossible to stop. Another area where research is important is the treatment of asthma. In recent years there has been a great increase in the number of sufferers and this has led to more investigations into the causes and how it can be controlled.

This boy suffers from asthma. He is using his inhaler to stop him having an attack. Scientific research is continuing to improve our understanding of this condition.

◣ IS YOUR LIFESTYLE HEALTHY?

To keep healthy, you should take some form of exercise every day, and eat a balanced diet (see page 9). You should also get plenty of sleep, because it gives your body the chance to renew and repair itself, and clean your teeth twice a day.

Keep a diary of your lifestyle for a week – does it match the suggestions made here?

MAPPING OUR GENES

Genes are made from a substance called DNA. This scientist is looking at a model of the DNA molecule on a computer.

In 2000 scientists announced that they had mapped the entire human genome – all the DNA in a human cell. The DNA carries a coded set of instructions for producing a human being.

Although scientists know what all the genes look like, they do not yet know what most of them do. If they can find out, they may find the causes of many illnesses, and why our bodies work less well as we get older.

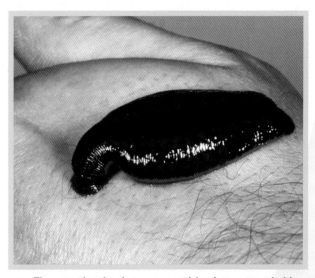

The way that leeches were used in the past probably made people more ill rather than helping them. However, today doctors are now using leeches once again, to control swelling during plastic surgery.

The Ancient Greeks believed that the body contained four fluids called humors. The humors were blood, phlegm, yellow bile and black bile. Blood was thought to be hot and too much of it caused fever. Phlegm was cold and too much caused colds. Yellow bile was dry and too much caused coughing and black bile was moist and caused people to feel sad or depressed. They believed that diseases developed if the four humours were not in balance. This idea was believed by doctors for over two thousand years, and they often used leeches to treat patients suffering from fevers. This was to draw out blood and restore the balance. It wasn't until much later that the work of Lind (page 9) and Pasteur (page 25) found that diet and microbes were the real cause of many diseases.

Claudius Galen (AD 129–216), a Greek doctor, dissected animals and believed that the insides of the human body were arranged in the same way.

Andreas Vesalius (1514–1564), a Flemish (Belgian) scientist, dissected human bodies and showed that Galen was wrong to think the insides of humans and animals were the same.

Gabriel Fallopius (1523–1562), an Italian scientist, made dissections of the human body and discovered that the ovaries in females were connected to the womb by tubes. They were named Fallopian tubes.

William Harvey (1578–1657), an English surgeon, discovered that the heart pumps the blood around the body.

James Lind (1716–1794), a Scottish doctor, discovered that including citrus fruits in the diet could prevent scurvy.

Edward Jenner (1749–1823), an English doctor, discovered that vaccination can protect the body from disease.

Rene Laennec (1781–1826), a French doctor, invented the stethoscope, which enabled doctors to listen to the heart and lungs more effectively.

William Beaumont (1785–1853), an American surgeon, made investigations on digestion by placing food through a hole in the stomach wall of one of his patients.

John Snow (1813–1858), an English doctor, showed that cholera could be spread by people drinking polluted water.

Crawford Long (1815–1878), an American doctor, used ether as an anaesthetic in an operation in 1842. This was the first time that an anaesthetic had been used in surgery.

Louis Pasteur (1822–1895), a French scientist, suggested that some microbes may cause disease.

Joseph Lister (1827–1912), an English surgeon, used carbolic acid as an antiseptic during surgery and found that it helped his patients to recover.

William Perkin (1838–1907), an English chemist, made dyes from substances in coal tar.

Robert Koch (1843–1910), a German scientist, discovered that cholera was caused by a microbe – a bacterium.

Wilhelm Roentgen (1845–1923), a German physicist, discovered X-rays in 1895. In 1896 he showed that they could be used to see the bones in the hand. They have been used for investigating inside the body ever since.

Paul Ehrlich (1854–1915), a German scientist, used dyes to see the structure of cells more clearly under the microscope.

Hans Berger (1873–1941), a German scientist, recorded the electrical activity of the brain with a device called an electroencephalogram (EEG).

Alexander Fleming (1881–1955), a Scottish scientist, performed investigations which led to the discovery of antibiotics.

GLOSSARY

antibiotics – chemicals developed to kill bacteria that cause disease. Some micro-organisms produce antibiotics.

bacteria – very small, single-celled living things (microbes) in which the DNA is not contained in a nucleus. They can cause disease.

cartilage – a tough, gristle like substance with a smooth surface that protects the joints in the body.

cell – a tiny packet of jelly-like cytoplasm enclosed in a thin membrane. Most cells have a nucleus containing DNA. The simplest life forms are single cells, but more complicated plants and animals are formed from millions of cells.

diagnose – to identify the cause of an illness by examining a patient and finding out their symptoms.

electrode – a wire that can conduct electricity.

enzyme – a chemical made by a cell that helps life processes such as digestion and respiration to happen faster.

fungi – living things such as mushrooms and moulds. Many fungi are microbes, and they feed on dead or living plants and animals. They reproduce by making large numbers of spores.

hormone – a chemical produced by organs in the body called glands. Hormones travel in the blood and affect the activity of various parts of the body.

immune – someone who is immune to a disease is safe from catching it.

minerals – simple chemicals found in soil that plants need for healthy growth. Humans also need minerals such as calcium in their diet (calcium gives us strong bones).

nutrients – substances in food that the body needs for energy, growth and good health.

ovaries – the organs in a female's body where the eggs are made.

parasite – an animal or plant that lives on or in the body of another living thing and gets their food from it. Some parasites cause disease.

protein – an important nutrient that supplies materials for the growth and repair of the body.

protists – microscopic living things (microbes) with bodies made from just a single cell. They may feed like animals or make food using light like plants.

respiration – the process of releasing energy from food to the cells in the body by taking oxygen into the blood and giving out carbon dioxide. This takes place when a living thing breathes.

spores – thousands of tiny 'seeds' produced by a fungus. New fungi grow from the spores.

testicles – the organs in a male's body that make sperm cells.

vaccine – a substance used to stimulate the body to protect itself from a disease.

viruses – tiny objects that do not have a cell structure. When they are introduced into a body they reproduce in its cells and cause tissue damage and disease.

INDEX